38

Great
Academic Language Builders

JOHN SEIDLITZ &
KATHLEEN KENFIELD

Seidlitz
EDUCATION

Published by Seidlitz Education
56 Via Regalo
San Clemente, CA 92673
wwwseidlitzeducation.com

Copyright © 2011 Canter Press

No part of this book may be reproduced in any form or by electronic or mechanical means, including photocopy, recording, scanning, or other, without prior permission from the publisher.

To obtain permission to use material from this work, please submit a written request to Seidlitz Education Permissions Department, 56 Via Regalo, San Clemente, CA 92673

For related titles and support materials visit www.seidlitzeducation.com.

11.13

Table of **Contents**

Introduction

This book is written for the many teachers we encounter during our training sessions who frequently echo this common refrain: "Our students struggle with academic language." It is no secret that teachers of English Language Learners, teachers of economically disadvantaged students, teachers in urban and rural districts, and teachers of average middle class students want to find a way to help their students build academic language skills. Simply put, they want to teach their students the language used in school, the language educators call academic language. In the educational world, these are the words and phrases used to communicate technical ideas and abstract concepts in any given subject area.

With this need in mind, we began to assemble activities from our training sessions that highlight academic language. This collection of activities is a gift all students can use. When students can speak, read, write, and think about academic concepts in a precise way, that is, when they have control over academic language, all doors to the future are wide open. As a result, students will be successful in college, in careers, and in life because they will be able to think critically and communicate effectively in any given situation.

How can we give the gift of academic language? Unfortunately, this gift doesn't come in a pretty package tied with a bow. Instead, it is a gift that teachers give over time by providing opportunities for students to practice language in authentic and meaningful ways. Student mastery of academic language is acquired from a variety of sources, with abundant reading topping the list. Research supports the idea that students who read abundantly have increased language development (Marzano, 2004; Krashen, 2000). Additionally, students learn academic language by listening to teachers who use the words in understandable and memorable ways, and they practice by speaking and writing with those words. This book encompasses all of the language arts strands in activities designed to enhance student acquisition of academic language.

Taking state standards into consideration, this book, and the activities in it, focus on complex concepts and higher-order thinking skills in every subject area. From mathematics to art, social studies to health, science to reading, and every subject in between, teachers will discover the powerful effect our academic language builders can have on students. Teaching students how to use academic language is a gift that students will unwrap throughout the year and for their entire lives.

38 Great Academic Language Builders is divided into four sections, each of which corresponds to a specific language domain. The first section, "Building Academic Vocabulary Skills," focuses on increasing student ability to understand content specific terms (such as *lymphocyte, isosceles, Manifest Destiny*) and the language of academic function (such as *persuading, analyzing,* and *summarizing*). This section also addresses transition words and phrases and provides word analysis instruction to help students become independent learners of new vocabulary. The second section, "Building Academic Conversation Skills," focuses on teacher and student interactions as well as student-to-student conversations. The activities in this section elevate oral communication in the classroom to include higher-order thinking as well as content-specific topics. Section three, "Building Academic Reading Skills," presents strategies to support students before, during, and after they encounter complex reading tasks in textbooks, primary sources, content-related articles, and the Internet. The final section, "Building Academic Writing Skills," helps students communicate their thoughts, summarize content area material, and refine their writing skills.

Each of the four sections in *38 Great Academic Language Builders* begins with a brief introduction followed by activities. The introductions provide background information, and they explain how the activities support academic language skills. Each activity in the book begins with a brief description that explains why and how to use the activity. Step-by-step directions for implementing the activity and specific examples follow each description.

From the start, our goal was to make a user-friendly resource to help teachers overcome common frustrations related to academic language instruction. Our final product is a book full of great activities that build academic language skills. The activities require minimal preparation; they are easy to implement; and students and teachers love them. In fact, teachers who use the activities in this book regularly find that students become skilled communicators and engaged learners. Ultimately, they find improved student achievement and confidence levels in these meaningful and authentic language lessons.

Building
Academic
Vocabulary
Skills

Many teachers ask this common question, "How can we help our students learn the vocabulary they need to know to understand what we are teaching?" In every math, science, social studies, and language arts class, teachers want to know how to help students build vocabulary. We all know that this is a real challenge. The challenge is complicated because we have to manage both the high volume of new words and the increasing complexity of those words in classrooms with students from very diverse learning backgrounds. The good news is that there are ways to teach students the words they need to know. The activities in this section are designed to give teachers some effective strategies for building the quality and quantity of academic language that students need to know and use regularly.

The activities in Building Academic Vocabulary Skills embrace three concepts: word knowledge, content-specific vocabulary, and general content-area academic words.

Activities like "Matching Morphemes" emphasize word knowledge. Morphemes are words, or small parts of words, that have meaning; these are words that cannot be divided. For example, "sub" means "under," "mar" refers to the sea, so "submarine" is "under the sea." Knowing the meanings of morphemes allows students to figure out the definitions of long, complex words. When students practice composing and deconstructing new and unfamiliar words through morphemes, words become puzzles they can solve.

The second focus of this section is content-specific vocabulary, or the core words, that students must understand in any given subject. Dutro and Moran (2003) labeled these "brick" words because they are the foundation of learning for each lesson, much like bricks are the basic component for building a house. Activities like "Describe, Describe, Draw" and "Lingo Bingo" offer innovative approaches to teaching "brick" words that are both engaging and effective.

The last focus of this section is instruction of what Dutro and Moran call "mortar" words, an often overlooked area in vocabulary teaching. They can be transition words like *first* or *second*, or words and phrases common in texts and tests, like *best represents* or *based upon*. Students need to know these words in order to fully comprehend what they read and hear. In continuing the analogy, Dutro and Moran call these process words "mortar" words because they cement and strengthen the core concepts. Much like a house of bricks without mortar would fall over, instruction focused only on key content vocabulary causes students to "fall over" academically. "Accidentally on Purpose" is an example of an ongoing activity that helps teachers use both concept and process words as a regular part of classroom instruction.

In addition to significantly increasing students' depth and breadth of academic vocabulary knowledge, these activities are focused, fun, and engaging! Students become excited about words, and they become highly skilled at using them to communicate. Not only do the skills in this section help students succeed in the classroom, but they can help students become eloquent speakers, persuasive writers, and confident readers throughout their lives.

Use the following activities to get your students ready to learn:

1. Interactive Word Wall
2. Introducing Morphemes
3. Morpheme Games
4. Say it Another Way Chart
5. Building Block Cards
6. Accidentally on Purpose
7. Teach Transition Words and Phrases
8. Quests for Vocabulary Building
9. Personal Dictionary
10. Vocabulary Quadrants
11. Describe, Describe, Draw
12. List, Group, Label
13. Lingo Bingo

1 Interactive Word Wall

Description

Why should you have words on your wall? The answer is simple. Walls can talk. In diverse classrooms, the walls are important scaffolds that help make the curriculum more accessible to students (Eyraud, Giles, Koenig, & Stoller, 2000). A Word Wall is, in essence, a list of key terms that can be elaborate or simple. The best word walls are not static. Instead, they change throughout the year. New words are added; and words that have been mastered are deleted. An effective Word Wall becomes a silent teacher. It is always there to remind students of the vocabulary words in their lessons, to give a quick definition for the words, to show the correct spelling of new vocabulary words, and to provide illustrations of the words. Word walls also remind us to have language moments whenever possible. We make the most of the interactive Word Wall when students use the words many times in written exercises and in classroom conversation. To create your class Word Wall, read the directions in the next column.

Directions

1. Determine which words to post on the Word Wall.

   * Select key concept words (the brick words) related to the unit under study as well as process, function, and transition words (the mortar words) like *represents* and *similar*.

   * Attach a visual to each word to provide additional support for students.

   * Change the Word Wall words often. Remove words that have been mastered. Add new words based on new content.

2. Organize the Word Wall words.

   * Think about the best organizational structure for your students. There are infinite ways to group words.

   * Words can be grouped alphabetically, by topic, or by content area (if you teach more than one content).

   * Other possibilities: Post high-frequency words, frequently misspelled words, transition words and phrases, "words we use all year," and "words in this unit."

3. Use the words on the Word Wall.

   * Do a daily "Word Walk 'n Talk." Select a handful of words from one of the lists to analyze, explore, and use in context. Challenge your students to use these words appropriately in sentences, and continually provide students with contextualized examples of academic terms.

   * Play "Guess the Word." Give clues to a posted Word Wall word and have students try to guess it. Your clues can be related to the following: number of syllables, parts of speech, sounds in the word, word within the word (morphemes), related words, definitions, descriptions, or sentence completions.

   * Refer to the Word Wall words during lessons and in conversation.

- Encourage students to use the words in whole class and student-to-student conversation.

- Praise students when you catch them using the Word Wall words.

- Require the use of specific words during a warm-up writing assignment or in a learning journal at the end of class.

- Specify a number of words to be used in section reviews, essays, or notes for class.

- Ask students to look for the words in printed sources outside the classroom, e.g., newspapers, magazines, or books. This shows a real-world connection to the vocabulary studied in class.

Additional Information
What if I don't have any space for a Word Wall?
Word Walls are just lists of words, and lists of words can fit anywhere. Obviously a bulletin board is a great place, but if one isn't available, here are some alternative locations:

- on the windows
- on the front of the teacher's desk
- on the side of the filing cabinet
- on closet doors
- above the whiteboard

Another option is to create a Movable Word List:
- Post words on a tri-fold board (think Science Fair).
- Place a cardboard box on top of a plastic turntable. Each side can represent a different word list that can be rotated as needed.
- Use large sheets of cardstock attached to coat hangers that can be displayed in the classroom when needed.
- Have students keep a personal version of the word lists in their notebooks.

Enhance your posters
Attach language to any posted visual in your classroom. A visual with no labels is nice, but not as powerful as one with the key words attached. Be sure students can read the words from their seats. Write the words using large print in an attention-grabbing color, style, shape, etc.

Student-created visuals
If there is not enough room on your walls to post definitions for each word, post a small visual that represents the words you study. Another effective way to give students additional exposure to new words is to have them draw the visual. Provide a stack of blank 5 x 7 index cards, and let students earn extra credit for creating visuals of your posted vocabulary. Select the best ones and post them right next to the words.

Final Note
The goal is for all students to be able to read any posted words from their seats. Some teacher's best efforts at creating Word Walls have been sabotaged by the glare of lights on laminated words, words written at distracting angles, or words posted on dark paper. As you post words, sit in a student's seat and look around to make sure that you can read all of the words on your walls.

2 Introducing Morphemes

Description

A morpheme is a small part of a word that has meaning. For example, the word "pre-reading" has three morphemes: "pre-," "read," and "-ing." These meaningful word parts are the building blocks of the academic vocabulary that students encounter in content area classrooms. Teaching morphemes gives students a tool for determining the meanings of unknown words as they encounter them in reading.

Directions: Part A

1. Become familiar with and practice using morphemes in your classroom.

2. Introduce the concept of morphemes to students.

   - Select 2-3 common examples that students encounter regularly, like "re-" (again), "anti-" (against), and "-ology" (the study of).

   - Brainstorm words with these morphemes, e.g., reflect, antibiotic, or geology, and show students how morphemes give information about the meaning of the whole word.

3. Teach morphemes in context by highlighting and defining morphemes found in content area and academic vocabulary. For example, "Look at the word 'chlorophyll'? Who knows what that means? That's right, it's the green material involved in photosynthesis. 'Chloro' means green and 'phyl' means leaf."

4. Post morphemes on the Word Wall and/or have students record them in their journals.

5. Challenge students with the "Spot the Morpheme" activity on the next page.

6. Refer to Appendix 1, "List of Latin and Greek Morphemes," to guide instruction.

Spot the Morpheme

Description

Learning to detect and decipher morphemes in words is the first step toward building a better vocabulary. Students can begin to learn morphemes by recognizing Latin and Greek roots. Have your students practice using the list below.

Directions: Part B

1. Have students examine the list below.

2. Ask students to underline the morphemes in each word.

3. Provide the "List of Latin and Greek Morphemes" in Appendix 1, and ask students to define each morpheme. Students can work in groups to complete this activity.

biography	homicide	supervisor
photography	herbicide	interstate
biology	herbivorous	intervene
antibiotic	carnivorous	circumnavigate
geology	voracious	submarine
geography	scripture	pseudonym
geometry	postscript	homonym

3 Morpheme Games

Description

Working with morphemes helps students realize that words can be "figured out" by carefully examining word parts. When students discover that the meaning of a morpheme can help them uncover the definition of a long and challenging word, listening, speaking, reading, and writing immediately become easier tasks to handle. Part A, "Morpheme Matching," lets students flex their morpheme muscles by using morphemes in a creative way. Part B, "Which one means...?" gives students advanced practice with morpheme recognition. The two activities can also be used to assess how well students understand various word parts.

Directions

PART A: Morpheme Matching

1. Provide a list of morphemes for students.

    • Begin with a list of a few morphemes, and increase the quantity on the list as students become more skilled at using them.

    • Always include morphemes related to current classroom vocabulary.

    • Include the definitions for the morphemes if they are new to students. If students have had multiple exposures to the morphemes, do not include definitions.

    • It may be helpful to divide the morpheme list into prefixes (morphemes that begin a word), roots (morphemes that form the base of a word), and suffixes (morphemes that end a word).

2. Ask students to create words using the morphemes from the list, either individually or in pairs. The words can be actual words or silly words.

3. Use the created words by:

    • writing a definition for each word based upon the meanings of the morphemes.

    • sharing the words with other students.

    • asking other students to guess the meaning of the created words.

Morpheme List
(without definitions)

pre-	read	-scope
auto-	hydro	-graph
photo-	geo	-ology
sub-	duo	-ist

Possible Student Responses:

1. Readology: the study of reading
2. Hydroscope: tool that observes water
3. Subgeology: the study of things under the Earth
4. Photoist: someone who believes in light
5. Autograph: writing about myself
6. Duoist: someone who does everything twice

PART B: Which one means..?

1. Compile a list of words that share a common morpheme. Display the list for students to see. Examples include:

    > _____scope
    >
    > microscope
    >
    > telescope
    >
    > gyroscope
    >
    > kaleidoscope
    >
    > periscope
    >
    > Pre_____
    >
    > preapprove
    >
    > precaution
    >
    > predetermine
    >
    > preface
    >
    > prepare
    >
    > ___bio___
    >
    > antibiotic
    >
    > biographer
    >
    > symbiotic
    >
    > microbiology
    >
    > biodegradable

2. Read the definition for one of the words on the list.

3. Instruct students to apply their knowledge of morphemes to connect the definition with the correct word. Provide the following sentence stem to improve the quality of responses: "I think the word is _____ because I know the morpheme _____ means ...."

4

Say it Another Way Chart

Description

This strategy enriches student vocabulary and increases the ability to describe phenomena and people through the use of academic language. For this activity, teachers provide sophisticated alternatives for high-frequency words and then give students multiple opportunities to use those alternatives. Using the "Say it Another Way Chart" helps students apply academic language they may not use in ordinary descriptions. It also provides an opportunity for students to be playful and have fun while engaging in academic conversation with low-frequency academic vocabulary.

Directions

1. Create a chart with two columns.* In the first column, list 8-15 high-frequency words that express judgments or emotions. In the second column, list six or more synonyms for each high-frequency word. (See the sample chart below.)
   *Be sure to make the chart large enough so that all students can see it clearly.

2. Ask students reflective questions about themselves or evaluative questions about people or phenomena encountered in academic texts or in their own lives. For example, "How did you feel when...." or "How did the main character behave when...."

3. Help students respond using the more advanced vocabulary from the posted chart. An excellent support is to provide a sentence stem for student responses. For example, after a science demonstration, the teacher might ask, "How would you describe the phenomena we just observed?" Students would respond with words from the chart using the following stem, "It seemed ___because..." or "During the demonstration, I felt ___ because..."

Say it another way...

angry	irritated	livid	irate	fuming	furious	heated
happy	elated	contented	ecstatic	joyous	pleased	delighted
big	gigantic	massive	huge	enormous	colossal	gargantuan
small	minute	petite	undersized	diminutive	infinitesimal	miniature
easy	effortless	basic	simple	trouble-free	painless	straight-forward
difficult	challenging	intricate	obscure	complex	taxing	demanding
strange	outlandish	odd	atypical	unusual	bizarre	eccentric

Building Block Cards

5

BUILDING ACADEMIC **VOCABULARY** SKILLS

Description

This activity (adapted from Zwiers, 2008) reinforces the concept that different kinds of words are needed to "build" academic understanding. Dutro and Moran (2003) highlighted the idea that there are two types of academic language: the key terms or "big idea" vocabulary from each lesson—called content-specific words—and the academic words—called non-content specific words—that surround the key terms. Content-specific words are usually bold faced or italicized in textbooks and teachers explicitly teach their meanings. Non-content specific words are general academic words that can be found in textbooks, tests, and conversations across all subject areas. They include transition words like *because,* signal words like *first* or *second,* and test-specific language such as *best represents* or *based upon.* Non-content specific words are often abstract, and without a clear definition, so the best way for students to learn these words is by using them. This activity gives students practice using the content-specific and non-content specific words they need to "build" academic understanding.

Directions

1. List up to five key vocabulary words ("bricks") from a current unit of study.

2. Have students (in pairs or groups) record each term on an index card. These are the brick cards.

3. Ask students to organize the brick cards in a way that makes sense to them.

4. Ask students to link the brick words together using academic language. Students write the academic language on "mortar" cards (or sentence strips) that cement the brick cards together.

5. Offer a list of "mortar" words and phrases to support students during this activity.

Example: ──────────────

Life Cycle of a Butterfly

CONTENT-SPECIFIC CARDS

metamorphosis pupa caterpillar

chrysalis butterfly

LIST OF NON-CONTENT SPECIFIC WORDS/PHRASES:
transforms • next • grows • inside • first changes into • begins • second • last • then process • forms • eats • resting • stage • is called

POSSIBLE STUDENT RESPONSES:

1. A butterfly begins as a caterpillar and then a chrysalis forms. It is now called a pupa and then breaks out as a butterfly. This process is called metamorphosis.

2. Metamorphosis is when a caterpillar transforms into a butterfly. First, it is a caterpillar, then a pupa inside a chrysalis, and last a butterfly.

6 Accidentally On Purpose

Description

This strategy intentionally incorporates academic language in a seemingly accidental way. In this activity, teachers can immerse students in academic language just by using it consistently in the classroom. Academic language is not just content-specific vocabulary; academic language can be used as transition and/or signal words. (See Appendix 2 for examples.) Classroom instruction is laden with academic language, and teachers can include those words during social and procedural conversations that occur throughout the school day. Teachers who seize the teachable moment to contextualize academic language for students make the language memorable. The more that teachers target key academic language "accidentally on purpose," the more students will begin to do the same.

Directions

1. Think about the key vocabulary words students have already been taught or will be exposed to during this lesson.

2. Ask yourself, "How can I teach this 'accidentally'" (in the context of my interactions with students)? It is acceptable if the usage is silly because it will be memorable for students.

3. Use academic language in your conversations with students. Some examples include:

Key word	Example of using the Key Word Accidentally on Purpose
foreshadow	"When I got out of my car this morning, I stepped right into a puddle. That *foreshadowed* a bad day."
climate	"My, the *climate* in this room is like the *climate* in Florida. It's warm!"
hypothesis	"Let's *hypothesize* what will be on the lunch menu."
significant	"What's the most *significant* thing that has ever happened to me? Let me tell you."

4. Create a "Word of the Day" by displaying a vocabulary word on the board or on the teacher herself (more fun!), and weave it into classroom conversation whenever possible. Praise students who use it correctly. For example, if you've chosen *fraction* as the word of the day, you could remark, "only a *fraction* of the class is paying attention right now!"

Teach Transition Words and Phrases

Description

Whether you call them *transition words and phrases, discourse markers*, or *signal words*, these academic relationship-indicators (*in contrast, moreover, consequently*) present a huge challenge for all of our students. These expressions are very difficult to define and to teach out of context, and they are often ignored in our zeal to teach subject area vocabulary. But since it is unlikely that our students will learn the appropriate use of these words from inference alone, we must teach these expressions, in all subject areas. They are key to both understanding academic language and to producing academic language when speaking and writing. So, how can we help our students with these essential bits of academic language? It's easy. Look at the chart below for the transitional expressions that can be organized by the cognitive task they represent. For example, the words in the second column express some kind of sequencing. Noting this classification is key to teaching these words effectively. On the next page, we offer three ways to teach signal and transition words and phrases explicitly.

Signal and Transition Words and Phrases

Description/List/ Generalization	Sequence	Comparison/Contrast	Cause and Effect Problem/Solution
for example	first, second, third	however	because
such as		but	since
to illustrate	in the first place	as well as	therefore
for instance		on the other hand	consequently
in addition	first of all	while	as a consequence
and	then	although	in order that
again	before	different from	so that
moreover	after	less than; fewer than	as a result
also, too	last	also, too	then
furthermore	meanwhile	like	if...then
another	now	though	thus
first of all	finally	much as	due to
second	for one thing	yet	accordingly
additionally	next	similarly	for this reason
not only...but also	subsequent(-ly)	similar to	
	late	whereas	
		as opposed to	
		still	
		in contrast	

7

Teach Transition Words and Phrases

Directions

The Language Moment

Any time you engage students in one of the cognitive tasks listed at the top of each column of the "Signal and Transition Words and Phrases" chart (description/list/generalization, sequence, comparison/contrast, cause and effect, problem/solution), continue by using the corresponding transition words. For example, after completing a step-by-step process activity such as a science lab, writers' workshop, or art project, continue by using words from the sequence column (Column 2). Say, "What did we do *first*? And *subsequently*, what did we do?" Or, if you have just compared or contrasted systems of government or characters in a story, use some compare/contrast transition words from the third column. Say, "*As opposed to* democracies, dictatorships discourage free expression." Or you could say, "Tim is a kind boy; *on the other hand*, Sally is mean."

The goal is to have students independently create sentences using the signal and transition words and phrases in the context of the material you have been studying. "Language Moments" begins as an oral language activity led by the teacher, but as students use the signal and transition words at a higher level, they can create sentences with the words. Explicitly modeling the use of signal and transition words in context, in a consistent manner, is the key to success.

Why does this method work? Simply put, your students have just experienced a sequential activity, or they have compared two characters, or they have learned about the causes and effects of the Civil War, and NOW their brains are primed to learn the signal and transition words and phrases that match the thinking they have done. Seize the teachable moment!

Post the Signal and Transition Words and Phrases

It is very helpful to post the "Signal and Transition Words and Phrases" chart in the classroom. Many teachers enlarge the chart on page 15 as a poster to remind students of these key words. Perhaps more importantly, it reminds the teacher to seize the teachable moment.

For example, if students have just compared and contrasted states in the union, have them write sentences using compare/contrast transition words. Simply point to the transition poster and take your students on a memorable Walk 'n Talk. Use examples like, "Montana is a huge state, while Rhode Island is a tiny one." "Similar to California, Florida has a long coastline."

Connecting Graphic Organizers with Signal and Transition Words and Phrases

Use academic language, especially signal and transition words and phrases, when working with graphic organizers. Seize the teachable moment after students complete a web, a timeline, a Venn Diagram, a flow chart, or another type of graphic organizer by asking yourself, "Can this be followed by a signal or transition word language moment?" Then engage students in conversation using signal and transition words. See the examples below.

Description/ List/ Generalization	Sequence	Compare/ Contrast	Cause and Effect Problem/ Solution
Our web shows many characteristics of _____. For example... Not only do we see_____, but we can also determine that... web	We see that _____ occurs first. Next, _____ happens. Before _____, then... _____ begins, later _____, and finally.... flow chart timeline cycle	_____ has _____ as opposed to _____ which has _____. _____ is similar to _____ because.... Venn diagram 3-part Venn diagram matrix or table	_____ occurred as a result of... _____ because... _____is due to... cause effect problem steps toward solution solution

8 Quests for Vocabulary Building

Description

Teachers find that scavenger hunt activities are valuable for helping students familiarize themselves with such things as a textbook, a chapter, the school, or the classroom. Additionally, scavenger hunt activities are perfect for teaching and reinforcing vocabulary, and there are many different types of quests students can enjoy while they learn.

Look at these examples:

Room Quest: This investigative activity helps students see their environment as a learning tool. Room Quests are useful for building and reinforcing academic vocabulary. They also help students become independent learners. During a Room Quest, students tune in to the wisdom and the language that teachers put on their walls, and they notice the important features of the classroom. Essentially, a Room Quest is an interactive approach that lets students see the many learning opportunities their classroom provides. For other ideas, see the Math Room Quest on the next page.

Text Quest: This is a very popular way to introduce students to any textbook. This activity is valuable because it not only teaches students how to use the textbook, but it leads students to meaningful encounters with academic vocabulary. Additionally, text quests help students understand the language of expository prose. For example, during the quest, students learn the meaning and purpose of the following terms: heading, margin, caption, graph, table, timeline, appendix, preface, table of contents, glossary, boldface, italics, review, summary, etc.
Text quests aren't just for the beginning of the year. They are effective when used multiple times throughout the year for various purposes.

Other examples of Quests are: Chapter Quest, Library Quest, Dictionary Quest, Phone Book Quest, and Internet Quest.

Directions

1. Determine your goal(s) for conducting the Quest. For example, your goals can be: to give students practice with newly-learned skills using objects within the room, to ensure that students know how to use the dictionary as a resource, or to teach students vocabulary from expository prose.

2. Write goal-related questions (depending on the type of quest you are conducting) that students can answer by searching the classroom, a textbook, the library, etc.

3. Distribute the questions to students (individually or in pairs).

Example of a Room Quest:

Math Room Quest

Work in pairs for this activity. Each pair will start at a different number.

1. What is the circumference of the globe we have in the classroom?

2. What is the square of the number of desks in the classroom?

3. Where can you find scratch paper in the classroom?

4. Which table in the classroom has the largest perimeter?

5. Look at the walls in the classroom. Find and list three math words that start with "c."

Example of a Text Quest:

Math Text Quest

1. Describe the picture on the cover of your textbook.

2. Why is the cover picture the best picture for your math textbook?

3. Write the definition of the word listed at the bottom of the first page of the glossary.

4. Find the answer key pages in the back of your textbook. Do they give the answers to all of the problems in the book? Why? Why not?

5. How does each chapter begin?

6. In every chapter, there are certain sections in brown boxes. Why are they different from the rest of the text?

7. How does each chapter end?

8. Sometimes you will find words in boldface (darker print). Why do you suppose these words are written in dark print?

9 Personal Dictionary

Description

Personal dictionaries are a combination of teacher-selected and student-selected vocabulary. Personal dictionaries enable students to focus on vocabulary that is significant to their learning, and they create a powerful sense of ownership of academic vocabulary for students. In addition, they can be used to assess focus words when students establish academic vocabulary development.

Directions

1. Provide students with a set of 3 x 5 index cards. (A set includes 5-10 index cards.) Punch a hole in the top corner of each card and use a metal ring to keep them together. Keep additional index cards available in the classroom so that students can add to their dictionaries as needed.

2. Have students write a new word on one side of the card. On the other side, have students write a definition for the word, an illustration for the word, and a sentence using the word.

3. Assess knowledge of personal dictionary words by providing study time for students in class, having students quiz one another about the words, or by conducting individual assessments with the students.

Which words belong in a personal dictionary?

There are two kinds of words that students record on the index cards in a personal dictionary: words selected by the teacher and words selected by the student.

Teacher selected words are typically words that teachers place on the Word Wall to help students understand content in a given context.

Student-selected words come from scans that students perform when reading unfamiliar material (see Scanning p.42). Students glance through the text looking for unfamiliar words, and teachers provide students with brief definitions of these words. Students record difficult words, and these words become part of their personal dictionary.

Vocabulary Quadrants
(Variations of the Frayer Model)

Description

Frederick Frayer's model for concept analysis helps students manipulate and master content vocabulary (Frayer, Frederick, & Klausmeier, 1969). This model consists of four boxes surrounding a key concept or vocabulary word. Frayer's original categories for the boxes are: definition, characteristics, examples, and non-examples. These categories help students gain a deeper understanding of academic terms. Our list on this page offers additional categories that serve the same purpose. Students enjoy filling in the boxes because small boxes are not as overwhelming as a single blank page. Changing the categories from time to time keeps this activity fresh and fun.

Directions

1. Have students create a Vocabulary Quadrant by folding a blank piece of paper into four parts. (Folding options and directions are on the next two pages.)

2. Select a category for each of the four boxes from the list below being mindful of the objective for each lesson as selections are made.

Possible Categories for the Vocabulary Quadrants boxes:

- Illustration of the word: Draw a picture of the word.

- Definition: Write the dictionary definition or a definition in the student's own words.

- My Own Sentence: Use the word in a sentence that relates directly (even if awkwardly) to the student's life. For example, "I was standing next to a plant when *photosynthesis* was happening;" or "My *Manifest Destiny* is to expand and take over my brother's half of our room."

- Related Words: List other words that have the same or related roots, morphemes, prefixes, suffixes, etc. For example: liberty/liberate/liberated/liberal—and from Spanish, libre.

- Is/Isn't: Complete the sentence stem "____ is..." and "____ isn't..." for the key word. For example: "Suspense is...jittery, nervous." "Suspense isn't... knowing for sure what will happen, relaxed." *Note: This category cannot be applied to all words.

- Personal Connection: Complete the sentence stem, "____ makes me think of ____ because..."

10

Vocabulary Quadrants
(Variations of the Frayer Model)

Creating a Vocabulary Quadrant:

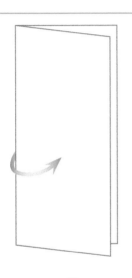

Option One: 2 Vocabulary Words
(one on each side of the paper)

1. Holding a sheet of paper lengthwise, fold it in half from left to right.

2. Fold it again from top to bottom.

3. Fold the point (which will be the center) into a triangular tab.

4. Opening the paper shows four boxes with a rhombus in the center.

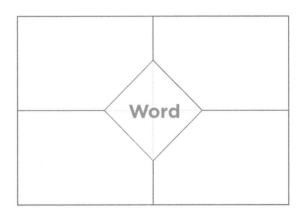

Option Two: 4 Vocabulary Words
(two on each side of a piece of paper)

1. Holding a piece of paper lengthwise, fold
    it in half from left to right.

2. Fold it in half again from top to bottom.

3. Fold it in half again from left to right.

4. Fold the point into a triangular tab.

5. Opening the paper shows two sets of
    four boxes with a rhombus in the center.

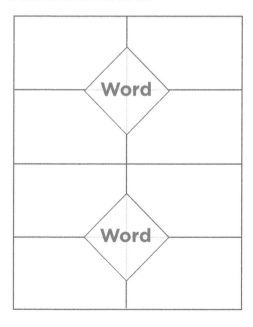

11

Describe, Describe, Draw

Description

This is a simple three-step strategy that teachers can use to build vocabulary in content area classes. It gives students multiple exposures to new academic vocabulary and allows them to learn from their peers as well as their teachers.

Directions

1. Describe a vocabulary word or term to students.

   · Select vocabulary words or terms that are content-focused and/or significant key words in a lesson or unit (Marzano, 2004).

   · Access prior knowledge, using visuals, and student-friendly language to make sure students have an understanding of the vocabulary word or term.

2. Have students describe the term in partners or groups.

   · Have students use their understanding of the teacher's description to describe the vocabulary word or term in their own words. Students can work individually or in groups to complete this activity.

   · Tell students that descriptions do not have to be complete.

   · Survey student work to make sure that descriptions accurately reflect the meaning of the vocabulary word or term.

   · Have student groups complete the descriptions and share them with the class. Ask students to add information they learn from other groups to their notes.

3. Have students draw a representation of the vocabulary word or term.

   · Ask students to create a drawing that represents the meaning of the vocabulary word or term, using icons, stick figures, or symbols to illustrate key ideas.

   · Note that student drawings can represent an example of the vocabulary word or term, the main idea of the word or term, or associations and connections to the word or term.

   · Have students work independently, in pairs, or in groups.

   · Instruct students to begin drawing only after the teacher has described the vocabulary word or term and the students have recorded accurate descriptions of the word or term (Marzano, 2004). Otherwise, students may create false associations that do not accurately reflect the meaning of key concepts. For example, the teacher can describe a "monarch" as the ruler of a country. If the student draws a measurement ruler with a crown on it, he/she has made a false association.

List, Group, Label

BUILDING ACADEMIC **VOCABULARY** SKILLS

Description

In this activity, students organize vocabulary in a variety of ways to gain a deeper understanding of academic terms (Taba, 1967). List, Group, Label helps students understand the relationships between academic concepts and the meaning of academic terms. It is important for teachers to remember to provide students with sufficient background knowledge in order to participate in List, Group, Label.

Directions

1. Give students a list of words, or have students brainstorm a list of words related to a given academic topic.

2. Ask students to copy the words or terms onto index cards with one card per word/term. Students can complete this step in groups.

3. Have students discuss the words and organize them into piles based on similarities. Each pile must have at least two cards.

4. Have students create a label for each pile that explains how the words within that pile are similar. Students might label by topic, by part of speech, by characteristic, etc.

5. Have students compare their labels to see how other groups organize the same information.

Example:

After discussing and sorting the terms into groups, students might create the following labels:

Shapes

Parts of a function

Representing functions

Types of functions

Included in a function

After finishing a unit on function in math, the teacher and students might generate the following list:

range	value
equality	inequality
expression	variable
graph	continuous
x and y	formula
quadrants	input
output	domain
lines	parabolas
f(x)	circles
ordered pairs	polynomial
vertical line test	

13 Lingo Bingo

Description

Lingo Bingo mirrors its generic counterpart with words instead of numbers. That means that students participate in the game by covering vocabulary words instead of numbers in each box. This activity is especially valuable in classrooms with students of varying ability levels. It allows high achievers to answer immediately, and it helps students who struggle to learn. Students love this activity because they think they are playing a game, but teachers know that they are learning key vocabulary.

Directions

1. Select key vocabulary words from a current unit of study. Have students write those words in the boxes of their bingo board at random. Use the bingo boards to begin play.

2. Read the dictionary definition of each vocabulary word on the bingo boards, one by one.

3. Tell students they are NOT to help each other as the teacher gives the clues the first time.

4. Define the word again, but scaffold the definition to make it easier to identify. If necessary, scaffold the definition yet again. The teacher's goal is to ensure that everyone understands. (See the list on the next page for scaffolding ideas.) Give all possible clues and hints.

5. Repeat the dictionary definition as the last clue.

6. Allow students to give each other whispered help, if necessary.

7. Have students cover or mark the appropriate box for each definition as it is called.

8. Have students call "BINGO" when they have covered a horizontal, a vertical, or a diagonal line of words. The first student(s) to make a "bingo" wins. Prizes are not necessary in this high-interest activity.

No-prep idea: Have students fold a piece of paper in half four times. The result is a 4 x 4 Bingo grid, ready to be filled in with the key words.

Scaffolding Ideas: What kinds of clues should be offered?

- Relate the word to a known word. (For the word *expansion*: "This word has to do with the way the United States grew toward the west in the 1800s. Sometimes when I do my homework, my papers do this on the kitchen table.")

- Relate the word to pop culture. (For the word *triangle:* "This word has the same number of sides as The Jonas Brothers has members.")

- Tell students that there's a hint in a morpheme within the word. (For the word *assimilation*: "There's a hint inside the word that means to become like someone else.")

- Tell students that the word rhymes with another word. (For the word fable: "The word rhymes with table.")

- Act out or give a gesture for the word. (For the word *preposition*, act out examples of this part of speech by placing a book under, in, on, by, or near a desk.)

Building
Academic
Conversation
Skills

Most teachers know that students like to talk to each other. With a little planning, teachers can capitalize on their students' desire to interact by guiding them toward specific language activities. In Building Academic Conversation Skills, the goal is to boost student knowledge of academic language. With that as a focus, the activities in this section are designed to make academic conversations a consistent part of daily instruction. With the addition of academic conversations, classrooms become a beehive of activity where teachers hear intelligent conversations and possibly even a heated debate or two. In addition, teachers see students come to class excited about sharing their ideas with each other. By incorporating academic discourse in the classroom, students learn to use sophisticated language when they think about content concepts.

The ten activities in this section scaffold one upon the other. The first five activities are strategies teachers can use across every subject area. The lessons require minimal planning, yet they dramatically increase the number and the depth of academic language opportunities students can have. The last five activities address speaking activities that further advance student ability to use academic language. All activities creatively approach the learning process. Choose from the activities in this section to help your students use academic conversation in your classroom.

Use the following activities to get your students ready to learn:

14. Banish "I Don't Know"

15. Speak in Complete Sentences

16. Q, Triple S, A

17. W.I.T. Elaboration Stems

18. Conversation Structures

19. Expert/Novice

20. News Show

21. Supported Interview

22. Prediction Café

14

Banish "I don't know"

BUILDING ACADEMIC **CONVERSATION SKILLS**

Description

Many students have grown accustomed to answering teacher questions by saying, "I don't know." In fact, all too often, this is a student's first response, and the reasons for the response are varied. Sometimes students really don't know the answer to the question; other times, they just don't want to participate. Too often, teachers accept an "I don't know" response and quickly move on to another student, or they offer the answer themselves. This practice trains students to be helpless and passive, and it communicates this idea: you are not expected to achieve. Instead of accepting an "I don't know" response, teachers can hold students accountable for responding in another, more productive way. When students are taught what to say, instead of "I don't know," they begin to move away from being helpless and passive to being independent and engaged in the classroom.

Directions

1. Create a large poster that lists alternatives to saying, "I don't know." Review each line of the poster with students.

> ### What to Say Instead of I Don't Know
>
> May I please have some more information?
> May I have some time to think?
> May I ask someone for help?
> Would you please repeat the question?
> Where can I find information about that?

2. Explain that saying, "I don't know" stands in the way of learning. Explain that "I don't know" is an obstacle that can be moved. Tell students they can refer to the poster, "What to Say Instead of I Don't Know" for a response that will direct them toward learning, instead of away from it.

3. Tell students they have two choices when asked a question by you: first, they can respond; second, they can request assistance by using one question from the poster. Either way, students must respond to questions without using, "I don't know."

4. Give specific examples for using the questions on the poster. For example: note the types of additional information you might provide, model think-aloud methods, show how to check with a classmate, or point to the resources within the classroom where students can find help.

5. Point to the poster when students give an "I don't know" response to a question. Be sure to hold students accountable during class discussions for responding without using "I don't know."

6. Teach students more specific ways to respond when they need help in new situations. For example, model ways for students to ask for help and clarification in a science lab, or have students ask a partner to explain something differently when they are confused or puzzled.

Speak in Complete Sentences

BUILDING ACADEMIC **CONVERSATION SKILLS**

Description

Communicating in complete sentences encourages students to use academic language. Imagine, for example, reviewing a multiple-choice math homework assignment with students. Think about the academic language opportunities that exist in this simple exercise. For instance, when the teacher asks for the answer to number one, the student responds by saying, "The figure that best represents a triangle is D," rather than just responding with the letter, "D." When students share their thoughts, answers, and questions using complete sentences, they practice using content area words and academic language. When they speak in complete sentences, they begin to write the same way. In addition, when they hear the words spoken in class by teachers and classmates, they are able to process content area vocabulary in context.

Directions

1. Explain the concept of sentence stems and provide some samples for students. (Also, see Sentence Starters below.)

2. Create and display a poster that says, "Please express your thoughts in complete sentences."

3. Teach students that one word answers or incomplete thoughts are for informal conversations, but for class, they need to use academic language. (Refer to the notes below to know the best situation for using complete sentences.) If students use an incomplete sentence as a reply, point to the poster and wait for a response with a complete sentence.

When should students speak in complete sentences?

It is not realistic that students respond using complete sentences every time they speak in class. There are two occasions, however, when it is appropriate to require students to respond with complete sentences: when reviewing numbered assignments, and when a sentence starter is provided (see below). As students become comfortable using complete sentences in these two instances, they will begin to use complete sentences on other occasions as well.

Numbered Assignments: Numbered assignments are sequential tasks that students need to complete, e.g., section reviews, chapter tests, multiple-choice assignments, math problems, etc. Whenever the teacher asks students to give answers out loud, they can expect students to respond with a complete sentence. This increases the opportunities to practice academic language, and it also increases the academic tone and quality of classroom discussions.

Sentence Starters: Sentence starters are short beginning phrases that students can use to construct complete sentences. For example, if the teacher asks, "What are two characteristics of the protagonist?" a sentence starter might be, "Two characteristics of the protagonist are..." Sentence starters (also called sentence stems) provide a way for students to communicate their thoughts using academic language. See Appendix 3 for a list of generic sentence starters teachers can use in all subject areas.

16

Q, Triple S, A

Description

Q, Triple S, A (or Question, Signal, Stem, Share, Assess) is an example of a structured conversation (Seidlitz & Perryman, 2011). In structured conversations, students share ideas and points of view with each other using content and language specified by the teacher. Student/student interaction focused on lesson concepts has been shown to have a significant effect on student achievement (Marzano, Pickering, & Pollock, 2001). In this activity, **every** student in the class participates using academic language, and it usually takes less than a minute to implement.

Directions

Question: Ask the class a question.

Signal: Ask students to give you a response signal when they are ready to answer the question. Examples of response signals include: showing thumbs up, giving a nod, crossing arms, etc.

Stem: Provide students with a Sentence Stem to use when answering a question.

Share: Give students the opportunity to share their responses with other students, in pairs, triads, or groups.

Assess: Determine the quality of student discussions and the level of student understanding. Teachers can assess students either by randomly selecting students to share out loud or by having all students write a response.

Here are some examples of Q, Triple S, A in different subjects:

Question	Signal	Stem	Share	Assess
(Math) What are some important things to remember when factoring equations?	Raise hand when ready to respond.	The most important thing to remember when factoring equations is... because...	Share in groups of three.	Randomly call on students.
(Social Studies) Do you support Sam Houston's position on secession? Why?	Thinker's chin*	I support/oppose Sam Houston's position because ...	Numbered Heads Together**	Numbered Heads Together continued**
(Science) What are some unusual characteristics of annelids?	Stand when ready.	The most unusual characteristic of annelids is... because...	Share in groups of two.	Randomly call on students.
(Language Arts) Is Stanley a hero?	Put your pen down when your response is written.	Evidence that shows Stanley is/is not a hero includes ...	Share answers with several partners.	Have students write their perspectives in response journals.

*Thinker's Chin: Students put fist on chin to indicate they are thinking; they remove the fist when they are ready to respond.

**Numbered Heads Together: Students discuss ideas in groups. Each person in the group is assigned a number. When the teacher solicits responses, she calls for a specific number to answer. For example, "Will all the "Ones" stand up and share their responses."

17 W.I.T. (Elaboration Stems)

BUILDING ACADEMIC **CONVERSATION SKILLS**

Description

Giving elaborate responses using academic language does not come naturally to most students. In fact, students need support in order to communicate in a detailed way. Providing students with simple prompts greatly increases their ability to elaborate during teacher-led discussions and peer interactions. Teaching and using elaboration stems gives students a tool that increases understanding during academic discussions (adapted from Seidlitz & Perryman, 2008).

Directions

1. Create and display the following chart:

> **W**hy do you think...?
>
> **I**s there another...
>
> **T**ell me more about ...

2. Use the prompts on the chart consistently during class discussions.

3. Encourage students to use the stems on the chart consistently during academic conversations.

Example:

Teacher: According to the primary source, why did Santa Anna vow "death to all?"

Monica: He wanted to scare the colonists into surrendering.

Teacher: Why do you think he wanted to scare them?

Monica: I think he wanted to avoid having a long war with them. He didn't want to lose.

Teacher: Is there another reason he vowed "death to all?"

Monica: Maybe he wanted to show his soldiers and other Mexicans that he was serious and wasn't going to back down.

Teacher: Tell me more about that.

Monica: Well the article says he held a council of war with his highest-ranking officers and that he wasn't going to take any prisoners. He wanted them all to know he wasn't playing around.

Conversation Structures

BUILDING ACADEMIC **CONVERSATION SKILLS**

Description

Classroom management can be tricky when you have twenty-five or more students working in groups. Sometimes it borders on chaotic, but with a little bit of planning, teachers can structure student interactions so they are controlled, productive, and fun. The ideas listed on this page give students multiple opportunities to discuss the academic concepts of each day's lesson in an organized way.

Directions

Lines of Communication: Students form two lines facing one another. The students in each row share ideas, review concepts, or ask one another questions. After the first discussion, one row moves, and the other row remains stationary so that each student now has a new partner (Kenfield; Echevarria, Vogt, & Short, 2008).

Carousel: Questions are posted in various stations around the room. Students are assigned to a group. Each group is assigned to a station and given a specified time to answer the questions at the station. Groups rotate around the room until everyone has answered all questions (Comments from CRISS, 1996).

Fold the Line: Students line up chronologically based on a predetermined characteristic such as height, age, number of pets, etc. The line then folds in half upon itself providing each student with a partner. Partners are then asked to formulate a response to a given task or question (Kagan, 1992).

Think, Pair, Share: The teacher asks a question and then provides wait time. The student formulates an answer, and then shares the answer with a partner. Afterward, selected students share their thoughts with the whole class (Lyman, 1981).

Inside/Outside Circle: Students form two concentric circles facing one another, an inside circle and an outside circle. Students then participate in a short, guided discussion or review with their partner. After the discussion, the outside circle rotates to the right while the inside circle remains still. All students now have a new partner for discussion (Kagan, 1990).

19

Expert/Novice

Description

In this activity, students get to be the expert who knows all the answers (adapted from Seidlitz & Perryman, 2008). Students enjoy this role-play so much they forget they are using academic language to review challenging concepts. Expert/Novice is a creative way to give students more practice talking about newly-learned concepts. This activity works particularly well with problem solving and with concepts involving a process.

Directions

1. Have pairs of students brainstorm a list of possible questions they might have about the topic. Teachers can also conduct a whole class discussion of possible questions to ensure that particular key concepts are included on the list.

2. Have partners prepare a short role-play where one student is the novice who doesn't know anything about the topic. The other student is the expert whose job is to teach the novice about the topic and to clarify any misconceptions.

3. Provide the following sentence starters to support partners as they create their role-plays:

Novice	Expert
How do you...?	The first step is...
What is...?	It is important to...
I don't understand why you...	Let me clarify that for you...

4. Have partners perform role-plays for the whole class.

News Show

BUILDING ACADEMIC **CONVERSATION SKILLS**

Description

The purpose of this activity is to give students a unique way to communicate their understanding of an academic topic. Rather than complete a worksheet or give an oral summary, students report about their new learning using the format of a news show.

Directions

1. Provide students with a list of key terms and concepts that must be included in the news show.

2. Explain and model each of the following parts of the News Show: *site location, reporting, in-studio guest interview(s),* and *commercials/advertisements.*

3. Have students work in pairs, triads, or groups to take on the role of producers and to create their own news show. In doing so, have them incorporate the key terms and concepts listed above.

4. Provide the following Sentence Starters to support groups as they produce their news show:

> ### News Show
> Good evening, Ladies and Gentlemen. Welcome to...
> We are broadcasting tonight from...
> And now, a word from our sponsors...
> We now go on location to...

5. Have each group perform their News Show for the class.

Examples of News Show Ideas:

Math: 3-Dimensional Figures	Social Studies: Boston Massacre	English Language Arts and Reading: Authors and Vocabulary Words
• Interviews with pyramids, cones, and cylinders with "A day in the life of...." theme.	• Interviews with Paul Revere, a Red Coat soldier, or King George (via satellite).	• Interview with a favorite author from a specific time period.
• Commercials for products that come in 3D shapes.	• On-location reports from King Street with bystander interviews.	• Commercials using vocabulary words as product names.
• On-location reports from an architect's latest uniquely shaped 3-D building.	• Advertisements calling all patriots to join the cause.	• On-location report with H.W. Longfellow, author of "Paul Revere's Ride."

21 Supported Interview

BUILDING ACADEMIC **CONVERSATION SKILLS**

Description

This activity requires students to think deeply about all the component parts of a complex topic or about the many decisions a character or historical figure faces in a given situation. During a Supported Interview, students use academic language to talk about lesson concepts from a perspective other than their own (Wilhelm, 2002). The Supported Interview encourages higher-order thinking skills, while providing built-in support for students who may encounter difficulty. The directions on this page outline the way to conduct a Supported Interview.

Directions

1. Select a complex concept, main character, or key historical figure to be interviewed. This person, idea, or thing will be the "Interviewee."

2. Have students use their notes, textbooks, novels, or any other available resources to find as much information about the "Interviewee" as possible.

3. Choose a student to become the Interviewee.

4. Select three students to sit in chairs directly behind the Interviewee. Their role is to provide support for the Interviewee while he/she is being interviewed. These students are called the "Support Team." The Interviewee can consult with his/her support team at any time. The support team can also stop the interview to talk to the Interviewee.

5. Have the rest of the students play the role of a relevant audience for the Interviewee. For example, if the Interviewee is Harriet Tubman, the audience may be a group of slaves about to start their journey on the Underground Railroad, or if the Interviewee is the Solar System, the audience may be the stars or the planets.

6. Have audience members ask questions to the Interviewee based on their notes using the following stems:

   Audience
   My question is…
   What's your view of…
   Can you explain why…
   Please clarify your position on…

7. Have the Interviewee respond to the audience questions, using the support team as needed. *Note: the Support Team is not allowed to respond directly to the audience, only the Interviewee.* The Interviewee can respond using the following stems:

   Interviewee
   Allow me a moment to respond…
   My opinion is…
   In response to your questions, I think…

Prediction Café
(Adapted from Zwiers, 2008)

BUILDING ACADEMIC **CONVERSATION SKILLS**

Description

During this activity, students talk about subject area material before they begin to read. During this pre-discussion, students will be exposed to many concepts from the text before they actually open the book. As discussions unfold, students can make predictions and determine the main idea of the text in advance. Students use many academic thinking skills including predicting, inferring, and synthesizing as they engage in Prediction Café. Students are also required to use academic language as they converse.

Directions

1. Select important headings, quotations, or captions (about 8 per class) from the text that students will read. Put them on separate strips of paper. Prepare one for each student. (Some students will have identical headings, quotations, or captions.)

2. Display the title of the text for all students to see.

3. Explain the goal of the activity, to make predictions and to form a main idea about the author's purpose for the text.

4. Give each student a strip of paper. Have students form pairs.

5. Have students read the strips of paper individually and make a prediction or guess about the meaning of the quotation as it relates to the predicted main idea/purpose of the overall text.

6. Provide the following sentence stems to facilitate student discussions:

   _____ makes me think that….
   I believe _____ because…
   I predict the main idea is …
   I think the author's purpose is…

7. Have the second partner share his/her sentence strip in the same way, and then have the partners discuss what they think the main idea of the text will be.

8. Have students find a different partner and repeat the process. Student predictions about the main idea should improve as they hear more and more quotations and predictions from other students.

9. Bring the class back together and lead a brief discussion about student predictions.

Building Academic Reading Skills

The make-up of any classroom usually includes a wide variety of student reading abilities. This means that teachers work hard to make sure everyone learns. Teachers know that for some students, grade level material is boring, while for others, that same material is incomprehensible. Compounding this challenging situation is the fact that reading is an internal process. Unlike speaking and writing, where the student's oral or written response is observable and measurable, students read inside their heads. Consequently, teachers may be unable to tell which students are struggling or which students are succeeding unless they have some sort of "output" activity after each reading task. To measure the output, teachers can structure a goal for the reading assignment and a way to measure that goal. The activities in Building Academic Reading Skills focus on giving students the support they need before, during, and after reading in order to successfully meet the academic goal for each reading task.

The first two activities, "Scanning" and "Language Anticipation Guides," are examples of strategies to use before students read text with dense academic language. These activities give students pre-exposure to unfamiliar vocabulary. Then, when students encounter the words in reading, they are prepared to make sense of them. Both activities reinforce newly-learned academic language because students have to interact with the words before and after the reading task.

The remaining activities in this section keep students focused and active while reading. During "Interactive Note Taking," students can dialogue with the text. In "Partner Reading," students share insights and confusing points as they read. In addition, the sentence starters in "Framed Summarization Strategies" minimize the struggle for readers while giving much needed practice with academic language.

The common denominator for all the Building Academic Reading Skills activities is to provide support before, during, and after reading so that students can successfully demonstrate their understanding of the assigned academic reading. Use the activities on this page to help your students.

.

Use the following activities to get your students ready to learn:

Scanning

Description

Scanning is a strategy used to teach students essential words appearing in new content, prior to reading. Pre-teaching terms prior to reading will enhance student comprehension of the material read and studied. Robert Marzano et al. (2001) cites research by Stahl and Fairbanks (1986) which demonstrates that student comprehension soars 33% when we pre-teach specific key terms to students prior to reading and learning. Pre-teaching unfamiliar words prior to reading can dramatically improve the reader's comprehension of the academic language found within texts.

Directions

1. Have students survey a text looking for unfamiliar words, starting at the bottom of a page and working up. Scanning the text backwards helps students quickly identify unfamiliar words without trying to read the material.

2. Ask students, as a class, to note the words they find. Then generate a list of three to ten unfamiliar terms from their lists.

3. Write short, student-friendly definitions for the terms, making sure to give definitions that match the way the word is used in the context of the passage. The *Longman English Dictionary* is a great source for student-friendly definitions.
   ** Note: The goal is to give students the information they need to understand the scan words they have listed. The goal is NOT for students to memorize or gain deep understanding of the words.

4. Practice pronouncing the terms with the students.

5. Ask students to read the passage.

6. Have students use the scan words to better understand classroom conversations and writing tasks related to the reading assignment.

Language Anticipation Guides

Description

This activity is a twist on the generic anticipation guide, which is a structured series of statements given to students before a lesson. To complete an ordinary anticipation guide, students read a statement and make a prediction as to whether the statement is true or false (Head & Readence, 1986). After instruction, students revisit the statements and reevaluate to see if they want to change their answers. Language Anticipation Guides mirror this process, but they focus primarily on the academic words and phrases students encounter within the text. This activity is particularly effective for words that are used differently in different subject areas, like "plot" in Language Arts vs. "plot" in Math. Even if students are familiar with one meaning of a word, they find that the word may appear as a different part of speech when used in a different context.

Directions

1. Select 3-8 key words or phrases found in a reading passage. (See the example at the end of this activity.)

2. Write a true/false statement for each key word that focuses on the meaning of the word as it is used in the passage.

3. Have students examine the statements and decide if the statements are true or false, prior to reading. This may be done individually, but it is a great opportunity for pairs to have an academic discussion as well.

4. Have students read the passage, taking note of the context surrounding each word from the Language Anticipation Guide.

5. Have students make changes to their true/false choices in light of any new understandings they formed while reading.

6. Conduct a brief, whole group discussion of each Language Anticipation Guide statement.

Language Anticipation Guides

Example:

Language Arts - *The Adventures of Huckleberry Finn*

Statement	Before reading	After reading
The phrase "winds up" means to finish, or end, something.	True / False	True / False
The word "awful" means terrible.	True / False	True / False
The word "interest" means something that you like or enjoy doing.	True / False	True / False
The word "rough" means difficult.	True / False	True / False

Text Passage:

Excerpt from *The Adventures of Huckleberry Finn* by Mark Twain

Now the way that the book winds up, is this: Tom and me found the money that the robbers hid in the cave, and it made us rich. We got six thousand dollars apiece—all gold. It was an awful sight of money when it was piled up. Well, Judge Thatcher, he took it and put it out at interest, and it fetched us a dollar a day apiece, all the year round—more than a body could tell what to do with. The Widow Douglas, she took me for her son, and allowed she would sivilize me; but it was rough living in the house all the time, considering how dismal regular and decent the widow was in all her ways; and so when I couldn't stand it no longer, I lit out (Twain, 1986 Revised Ed.).

Partner Reading

BUILDING ACADEMIC **READING SKILLS**

Description

Having a classroom composed of students with widely varied reading abilities can be difficult when assigning reading tasks. While some students will be able to comprehend the material easily, not all students will be able to do so. Partner reading can help minimize this problem, and when executed correctly it can have a significant positive effect on both students in the partnership. The listener gains access to important academic concepts that may be written above an individual reading ability. The reader gains deeper understanding of the key ideas and increases fluency. In addition, the social component of reading with someone else boosts the level of reading engagement for both students.

Directions

1. Assign the text and the partnerships. Be sure to match students so that there is at least one on- or above-level reader within each partnership.

2. Establish a goal for the reading task.* For example, "Identify two characteristics for each phase of the lunar cycle," or "Determine why Little Ann and Old Dan are main characters."
   *Setting the purpose for reading tells each partner there is a specific job to do, and it sets an academic tone for the discussion.

3. Put partners together to decide how they will structure the reading task.* For example, they may alternate reading each paragraph, page, or they may divide the assignment in half.
   *Allowing student choice about reading tasks helps partners feel safe enough to take risks and receive help from peers.

4. Have partners read the text and stop every 2-3 paragraphs to discuss the information. Teachers can support those conversations by providing the following stems:

   You read about…
   I'm wondering…
   I think that…
   What you just read relates to our goal because…

26 Sentence Sort

Description

Sentence sorts help students analyze academic language structures and the various ways authors communicate their ideas. To begin, teachers provide students with several sentences and ask them to categorize them according to various criteria. This activity requires students to interpret each word in the sentence as they determine how to sort them. Sentence sorting is most effective when students sort in pairs or triads because they have to justify, to their partner(s), why a sentence belongs in a specific category. The tactile nature of sorting increases student engagement as well.

Directions

1. Select sentences from the textbook, a piece of literature, or even from primary source material. Print the sentences on strips of paper and put them in an envelope. Give each pair/group one envelope.

2. Explain the type of sort students should conduct: open or closed. In an open sort, students are free to categorize the sentences in any way they want. In a closed sort, the teacher creates the categories. Here are some examples of closed sort categories:

   • Descriptive sentences

   • Complex vs. simple sentences

   • Sentences that connect ideas vs. compare ideas

   • Sentences with opposing ideas

   • Main ideas vs. supporting details

   • Fact vs. opinion

   • True vs. false sentences

3. Have students sort the sentences according to the predetermined criteria.

4. Debrief the sentence sort as a whole group. Record any accurate generalizations students discovered during the sort. For example, if students conducted a complex vs. simple sentence sort, they may determine that, "All the complex sentences included either a conjunction or a relative pronoun."

Framed Summarization Strategies

BUILDING ACADEMIC **READING SKILLS**

Description

Framed summarization strategies help students organize their thinking as they attempt to summarize text. Writing a skilled summary is a difficult task. It requires students to eliminate nonessential information, identify key points, and rewrite ideas in an organized way. The frames on this page help students make sense of the various types of academic texts they encounter. They also provide students with some of the academic language necessary to skillfully summarize the content.

Directions

Framed Oral Recap: This is an oral review involving two students using sentence starters. Students are given stems like the ones below. After reading an assigned text, they prepare responses using the stems and then pair up with a partner to discuss what they have learned (Zwiers, 2008).

> After reading this, I realized...
> Now I know...
> The most significant thing I learned while reading was...

Summarization Frames: Students are given a specific set of sentence frames to structure summaries of academic texts (Adapted from Marzano et al., 2001). The sentence frames should be specific to the type of text assigned.

Sample Summarization Frames

For nonfiction informational text:

- This is about...
- The author narrows the topic by discussing...
- Some examples the author gave about _____ included....

For argumentative text:

- The author believes...
- The author supports his belief by...
- Some ideas that go against the author's claim include...
- The author refutes those claims by...

For problem/solution articles:

- The problem is...
- A possible solution is...
- Another possible solution is...
- Yet another possible solution is...
- The author probably thinks the best solution is...

BUILDING ACADEMIC **READING SKILLS**
Framed Summarization Strategies

Fist Summaries: Students summarize a text by stating five things they remember about a passage, numbering off on their fingers as they state each one.

Five W's: A 5W summary can be used for an expository text. Students simply answer the basic questions who, what, where, when, and why about an informational text.

Somebody, Wanted, But, So, Then: Students include "somebody, wanted, but, so, then" in order to create a summary of a narrative text (Macon, Bewell, & Vogt, 1991). For example, if students were writing a summary of the American Revolution, they would make the American colonists the "somebody." The summary might be, "The colonists *wanted* to have equal representation in Parliament and have their civil rights respected, *but* the British refused to grant their demands, *so* they began a revolution. *Then* they became independent."

Cloze
Activities

BUILDING ACADEMIC **READING SKILLS**

Description

A Cloze activity is a text or reading passage that is missing words. To prepare a cloze exercise, the teacher intentionally deletes either significant content area terms or other academic words that challenge students, like transition words. Cloze activities help students practice academic vocabulary, and they help teachers assess student knowledge and comprehension of content area terms (Taylor, 1953; Gibbons, 2002). Cloze activities that focus on non-content area terms are also helpful because they give students an opportunity to examine several ways to use transition terms as well as terms that show relationships and significance. Good cloze activities will often result in more than one correct answer. For example, students may choose to use the word "important" instead of the word "significant," or they may use a phrase such as "on the other hand" rather than the word "however."

Directions

1. Select an appropriate text, relative to the content being taught that day in class. Excerpts can be taken from textbooks, trade books, magazines, and/or Internet articles.

2. Delete significant content area terms or transition words. Have students determine what words should fill the blanks. See the examples below.

For example, the original text might read:

One of the significant causes of the Great Depression was the collapse of the stock market in 1929. However, there were other significant causes as well. One of these was rampant property speculation in the western part of the United States.

To focus on content area vocabulary, delete "Great Depression," "stock market," and "speculation."

One of the significant causes of the _____ was the collapse of the _____ in 1929. However, there were other significant causes as well. One of these was rampant property _____ in the western part of the United States.

To focus on non-content area terms, delete "significant," "however," and "as well."

One of the _____ causes of the Great Depression was the collapse of the stock market in 1929. _____, there were other significant causes _____. One of these was rampant property speculation in the western part of the United States.

---

3. Each student reads a copy of the cloze text and fills in the blanks. A word bank offers additional support for this activity.

29 Interactive Note Taking

Description

The principle behind any note taking activity is for students to record small bits of information that they read or hear in order to help them understand and remember what they learn. Interactive note taking propels this process a step further by giving students space to record their thoughts, questions, and reactions about the new information. Students are no longer just copying key words or phrases; instead they are interacting with the text and thinking about new academic concepts. Several options for interactive note taking are listed on this page.

Directions

Cornell Notes: In this method, students divide their papers into two unequal sections. In the large column, students take traditional notes in modified outline form. In the smaller column, students write key vocabulary terms and questions (Pauk, 1962).

Double Entry Journals: Students write reflectively about texts using a two-column journal. In one column, students record words, phrases, or ideas that they found interesting or significant. In the other column, students write the reasons they found them significant or ways they could use them in their own writing (Samway, 2006).

Episodic Notes: This method works well when new information is formatted in sections, stages, or when it explains a process. To begin, students fold a piece of paper into two columns. On the left side, students draw a representation of what they learned in the first section or chunk of text and record their notes about that section on the right side. They repeat this process for each section (Burke, 2002).

Field Notes: Students take notes and write in a journal, adding reflections about what they are learning and experiencing. Field journals can be written or drawn and should be content focused. They can contain both social and academic language (Samway, 2006).

Idea Bookmarks: Students take reflective notes on bookmark pieces of paper; the bookmarks include quotations, observations, and words that strike the reader as interesting or effective. The bookmarks can be divided into boxes to add more quotations and page numbers (Samway, 2006).

SQP2RS
"Squeepers"

Description

SQP2RS stands for survey, question, predict, read, respond, and summarize. In this activity, students use cognitive and metacognitive strategies to process non-fiction text. The step-by-step process outlined on the right requires students to pay attention to text features as well as their own thinking processes. As they do this, they increase their ability to comprehend academic language in text.

Directions

1. Survey: Students scan the visuals, headings, and other text features.

2. Question: Students write questions they think might be answered when they read the text.

3. Predict: Students write predictions about what they might learn while reading.

4. Read: Students read the text.

5. Respond: Students revisit their questions and record any answers they discovered while reading. Students also think about the strategies they used to help them understand what they read. Teachers can also provide a specific stem for response time as well.

6. Summarize: Students restate key concepts either individually or in groups.

Building
Academic
Writing
Skills

Academic writing can be difficult for students, but it does not have to be.
To make academic writing accessible and enjoyable for students, give them a perspective from which to write. The easiest and most obvious point of view from which students can write is their own.

The first three activities included in Building Academic Writing Skills provide students with opportunities to write their own thoughts and questions about academic topics. While they do this, students engage in their learning as they make applications to real life situations.

The remaining five activities are all a variety of "perspective-based writing," or writing from an assigned point-of-view using specific academic language. During perspective-based writing, students may take on the role of an historical figure, an inanimate object, or even an expert within a field of study. When students write from these perspectives, they must think at higher levels and engage in academic discourse from a variety of points of view. Teachers often see students who were previously uncomfortable and unskilled when writing non-narrative text in content area classes become motivated and confident writers during perspective-based writing activities.

To build academic writing skills, teachers can provide the right amount of support and modeling. Students benefit from seeing a teacher model the writing task before they tackle the assignment on their own. Even when students are at a point where they feel prepared to write independently, there are still support systems that can be built into a lesson. Providing academic word lists and sentence starters during writing empowers students and helps them become successful. Try the following academic writing skills activities with your students.

Use the following activities to get your students ready to learn:

31. Chat Room

32. Ticket Out

33. Interactive Journals

34. Writing Windows

35. Letter/Response

36. Written Conversation

37. Fortune/Misfortune

38. Genre Imitation

31

Chat Room

Description

This writing activity helps students transition from everyday social language to writing with academic language. While writing, it is common for students to communicate their understanding of a topic using generic, high-frequency words. The goal of this activity is to draw students' attention to and increase the complexity of the type of language they use when writing. Students enjoy the "pop culture" aspect of this activity.

Directions

1. Give students an academic term or concept and a paper outline of a computer screen.

2. Have students describe the term/concept as if they were instant messaging a friend or sending a text message. Students record their descriptions on the computer screen.

3. Have students pair up and switch screens. Partners rewrite the description using academic language and a more formal tone, deleting any slang and abbreviations. Providing sentence starters will help support students during this part of the activity.

Example:

A hypothesis is when you guess why stuff happens. You have to be able to check to see if it is right.

A hypothesis is a way to measure and explain a phenomenon. Conducting an experiment can either prove or disprove a hypothesis.

Ticket Out

BUILDING ACADEMIC **WRITING SKILLS**

Description

This quick and straight forward activity requires minimal preparation, but when implemented as a regular part of daily lessons, it has an incredible impact on the quality of written responses. The "Ticket Out" asks students to write something about the academic focus of the day's lesson. This gives them immediate practice using the academic language that was just introduced. It also gives teachers an excellent way to check student understanding, and it provides tailor-made content for the next day's lesson.

Directions

1. Ask students to reflect on what they learned at the end of the lesson or class period. Have students write a "Ticket-Out" using a sentence stem on a sticky note. A "Ticket Out" can be open-ended or very specific. Here are some examples:

   • I learned something new today, and it is...

   • I think...

   • What I learned today reminds me of...

   • The term _____ means...

   • I am still confused about...

   • Tomorrow I hope to find out...

   • The main idea of _____ is....

   • One characteristic of _____ is....

   • Change the content objective for the day into a sentence stem to make a very specific "ticket out."

2. Collect the sticky notes and review them.

3. Use student responses to guide the next lesson.

4. Use an alternative "Ticket Out" approach. Have students record the sentence stems in their journals for future reference or for upcoming writing assignments.

33 Interactive Journals

Description

Interactive journals build students' academic language skills in a non-threatening way. In journals, students write about academic concepts they share with another student and/or the teacher. The tone of journaling is more conversational than it is in formal writing assignments, and this helps students feel comfortable using content-specific terminology.

Directions

1. Have students build background knowledge through academic discussion and visuals when beginning to learn new academic concepts.

2. Ask students to begin journaling by writing a reflection using a sentence starter specific to the content being studied in class. For example, a sentence starter for a study of various land forms might be, "The characteristics of a plateau are…" A sentence starter for a study of quadratic equations might be, "To solve a problem using the quadratic equation, first I …"

3. Have students share their journal reflection with another student. The second student writes a response in the first student's journal, asking any questions or making any appropriate comments related to the academic topic. Some example sentence starters for responding are:

   What you wrote was interesting because…
   I also thought…
   I like the way you…
   I'm wondering why…
   When you wrote _____, it made me think of …

4. Have students return the journals to their owners. The teacher can collect the journals and write a reflection to the student as well.

Writing
Windows

BUILDING ACADEMIC **WRITING SKILLS**

Description

This activity asks groups of students to respond to pictures or photos related to an academic concept. The images reflect different perspectives which deepen student understanding of the topic. Students respond well to this activity because the visual representation helps make the concept more comprehensible, and there is an element of secrecy that they love. In "Writing Windows," students brainstorm lists of words specific to the content being studied, and these can be referenced while writing. The lists inspire and motivate students when they begin to write their descriptions.

Directions

1. Organize students into groups of four. Give each student in the group a folder containing a different image on the current topic of study and a 5" x 8" index card.

2. Ask students to keep their images a secret from others in their group.

3. Have students record their responses to the following directions on the index card:

   • List everything in the image.

   • List adjectives that describe the objects in the image.

   • List all action words (verbs) in the image.

   • Pencils down. Close your eyes and imagine yourself in your image. Look all around.

   • What else can you see? hear? smell? taste? touch? What are the people in the image wearing and saying? Record your thoughts.

4. Give students a second index card with a sentence stem that corresponds to the image. Ask them to use the stem to write a paragraph from a perspective within the image.

5. Give students time to share their writing with the others in their groups. After they share, students show the image in their folders to the group members.

Example Images/Sentence Stems for Erosion Unit:

Sentence Stem: "We had been hard at work for days trying to finish..."

Sentence Stem: "I've grown vegetables on this land for over 80 years, but..."

Sentence Stem: "This state-of-the-art erosion control blanket can help you by..."

Sentence Stem: "I've been driving this same freeway to work every day and was shocked when I realized this is what caused my flat tire. I think..."

Letter/
Response

Description

This activity is very much like a chapter review or paragraph summary with a small twist. In Letter/Response, students have a chance to inject their own curiosity and creativity while they use academic language in writing.

Directions

1. Have students write a question for a specific character/object after studying a historical era, piece of literature, natural phenomenon, or organism. For example, after a unit on the Civil War, students might select Robert E. Lee. After a unit on states of matter, students might be curious about "liquids."

2. Have students write a letter to their selected character/object, asking about their lives, important decisions they made, specific characteristics they have, and/or interesting personal qualities they possess.

3. Ask students to exchange letters with other students and have them write a response to the letter they receive.

4. Have students give the letter and the response back to the original writer, and have them discuss whether they agree or disagree with how the individual responded to their letter.

36 Written Conversation

Description

Finally, students get to pass notes to each other and not get in trouble for it! This activity is a quick writing task designed to practice using academic language from any given topic, using two different perspectives. Pairs of students can engage in a "Written Conversation" in the middle or the end of a unit of study.

Directions

1. Have students brainstorm the attitudes and beliefs of two characters or objects related to a current unit of study in any subject area.

2. Ask students to imagine something one character or object might say to the other if given the chance.

Sentence Frames for Brainstorming...
(Character/Object) probably believes...
(Character/Object) might say...
One word/phrase (Character/Object) might say is...

3. Have students form partnerships, as partner A and partner B to express points of view. Examples include:

Subject Area	Student A Point-of-View	Student B Point-of-View
Social Studies	George Washington	King George III
Science	Vein	Artery
Math	Best way to solve the word problem is making a chart	Best way to solve the word problem is computation
Language Arts	Protagonist	Antagonist

4. Have Partner A begin by writing a short note to Partner B. Have Partner B read the note and write a short response on the same piece of paper and pass it back to Partner A. Have students continue this exchange for 10 minutes.

Sentence Frames for Notes
Dear _____, I'm writing to express my opinion about...
You might want to consider the fact that...
I must respectfully disagree with your thoughts about...
I see we agree about...

5. Have students discuss the note as partners and then with the whole class.

Fortune/ Misfortune

BUILDING ACADEMIC **WRITING SKILLS**

Description

This activity places students in the midst of the content they are studying. They write from a first-person perspective about the academic concept and are faced with making decisions that may have a positive or negative effect. Students gain deeper levels of understanding because they are personally invested in the topic.

Directions

1. Have students read about and discuss a historical or real life situation in class that reflects the academic concepts of a current lesson. Here are some examples:

Subject Area	Situation
Math	• conducting a clearance sale at a retail store • marking down all items
Language Arts	• Scout and Jim deciding to knock on Boo Radley's door
Science	• getting ready to conduct a mission to Outer Space
Social Studies	• settling in Jamestown in 1607

2. Brainstorm a list of items that would be important to have in a particular situation.

3. Brainstorm a list of possible fortunes and misfortunes that could happen in that situation. The teacher writes these possibilities on index cards.

4. Have students choose and list six to ten items from the brainstormed list that they might need during a particular situation.

5. Have students write a short paragraph from the first-person perspective describing a day in their situation. Students can use the items they chose from the brainstormed list.

6. Select a fortune or misfortune card randomly from the deck.

7. Ask students to write a new paragraph describing how they responded to the fortune or misfortune. Continue to draw additional fortune/misfortune cards, and have students write new response paragraphs.

8. Have students share their writing with partners or as a whole class to conclude this assignment.

38 Genre Imitation

Description

In this strategy, students read high quality selections from a given genre of writing. Genres can include categories such as fairy tales, letters to the editor, advertisements, lab procedures, word problems, informational pamphlets, textbooks, etc. Students analyze and then practice writing in one genre. Writing from within a genre using a step-by-step process helps students use academic language in the same way as professional writers. This activity is particularly helpful for word problems in math and state assessment test questions in all subjects.

Directions

1. Provide students with genre samples.

2. Have students identify and list significant and recurring phrases within the genre.

3. Identify text patterns (e.g., What happens in the beginning, the middle, and the end of the text?) and text structures (e.g., Do authors of this genre use bold, text boxes, and/or illustrations, etc.?).

4. Create a sample of writing within the genre using significant recurring phrases, patterns, and structures, as a class.

5. Create a sample of genre writing independently.

Appendices and Bibliography

List of Latin and Greek Morphemes

Prefixes

a, ab	away, from, apart, away from	avert, astringent, abnormal, abstain, ablation, abduct, abscission
a, an	not, without	asymmetrical, amoral, anachronism
ad	to, toward	adhesion, adjoin
ambi, amphi	both	amphitheater, ambiguous, ambivalent
ante	before	antecedent, anterior, anteroom
anti	against	antiaircraft, antipathy, anticlimax
bene	good	benevolence, beneficent, benefit, benevolent
circum	around, round, surrounding	circumstance, circumference, circumscribe, circumnavigate
con, com, co	together, with	continue, communal, connection, cooperation, company
contra, counter	against, opposed to	contraindicate, contradiction, countermeasure, counterplot, counterpoint
de	down from, away from, reverse	departure, derailment, demerit, debrief
dia	through	dialectic, dialogue, diagnosis, diameter, diagonal
dis	opposite of, away	disinherit, disperse, disenfranchise, dismissal
dys	ill, bad, impaired, difficult	dysplasia, dysfunctional, dyslexia
epi	upon, above	epidemic, epigram, epitaph, epicenter, epidermis, epilogue
ex	out, out of, away from, formerly	exoskeleton, exotic, exterior, exit, exclusion
fore	in front	forehead, forecast, foreshadow, foreclose, forebode, forearm

hyper	over, above, beyond, excessively	hyperactive, hypersensitive, hypersonic, hyperventilate
hypo	under, beneath, below	hypochondriac, hypothermia, hypodermic, hypodermal
il	not	illiterate, illegal, illogical, illusion
in	in, into, within	incision, insertion, inclusion
in-	not	incredible, inhospitable, infinite, infinitesimal, incapable
inter-	between, among	interact, interpret, intervene, intercept, interstate
intra, intro	within	intramurals, intravenous, introduction, introspection
luc	light	lucent, lucid, translucent
mega-	large, great	megawatt, megahertz, megaphone, megabyte
mis	wrong(ly), incorrect(ly)	misunderstood, mistake, misspell, misprint, miscalculate
multi-	many	multisyllabic, multicolored, multiply, multitude, multivitamin
neo-	new	neophyte, Neolithic, neonatal, neoplasm
non-	not	nonentity, nonpayment, nonprofessional, noninvasive, nonsense
nov-	new	novel, novelist, novelty, novice
omni-	all	omnipresent, omnipotent, omniscient
pan-	all	pandemic, panacea, panorama, pantheism, panic
per-	through, throughout, over, large, high	perceive, perfuse, pervade, pervasive, perfect
peri	around	peritoneum, periscope, perimeter
poly-	many	polygon, polygamy, polyester, polyethylene, polyglot, polytechnic, polysyllabic

Prefixes

post-	after	postpone, postscript, postoperative, postnasal, postpartum, post-war
pre-	before	preview, premier, premium, preface, prewar
prim-	first	primer, prime, primary, primitive
pro-	in favor of, forward, in place of	probiotics, project, projectile, pronoun
proto-	first	protoplasm, prototype, protocol, proton
re-	back, again	repetitive, retraction, revert, repetition, retrace, refurbish, regenerate
retro-	back, backward	retrospect, retroactive, retrograde, retrorocket
se-	away, apart	segregation, seclusion, secession, sequester
sub-	under, below	subterfuge, submarine, subterranean
super	over, above, beyond	superfluous, supervisory
sym-, syn-	together, with	symbiotic, symphony, symmetry, symbol, symptom, synthesis, synchronize, synonym, synonymous
trans-	across, over	transport, transcend, transition, translate, transmission
ultra	excessively	ultramodern, ultrasound, ultralight, ultraviolet

Roots

acer-, acr-	sharp, bitter	acerbic, acid, acrid, acerbate
alter-	other	alter ego, alternative, alternate
ambul-	walk	ambulatory, ambulance, amble, somnambular
amor	love	amiable, enamored, amorous
annu, enni	ear	annual, annually, anniversary, biennial, centennial, perennial
anthropo-	man	misanthrope, philanthropy, anthropology
aqua	water	aqueduct, aqueous, aquarium
arch	ruler, chief, first	archdiocese, archenemy, monarch, anarchy
aster	star	astronomy, asterisk, astronaut
aud, audit	hear, listen to	audiology, auditorium, audition, audience
bene	good	benefactor, benevolent, benign, benediction
bibl-	book	bibliography, bibliophile, Bible
bio-	life	biome, biometrics, biology, biography, biopic
calor-	heat	caloric, calorie
cap-	take, hold	capable, capture
capit, capt	head, chief, leader	captain, caption, capital, captor
cardi-	heart	cardiovascular, cardiogram, cardiology, cardiac
carn-	flesh	carnal, carnivorous, incarnate, reincarnation
caus, caut	burn	caustic, cauldron, cauterize, holocaust
cause, cuse ,cus	cause, motive	excuse, accusation, because, cause

cede, cess	move, yield	procedure, concede, recede, precede, accede, success
chrom-	color	chromosome, polychrome, chromatic
chron-	time	chronology, synchronize, chronicle, chronological
clud	shut	conclude, include, exclude
corp, corpor	body	corporation, corpse, corporal
crat, cracy	power, rule	democrat, aristocrat, democracy, theocracy
cred-	believe	credit, credible, incredible, credo
crux, cruc	cross	crucify, crucifix, crucial, crucible, crux
crypt	secret, hidden	crypt, cryptic, cryptogram
culpa	blame	culprit, culpable
cur, curs	run, course	concurrent, current, incur, occur, precursor, cursive, cursor
dem-	people	epidemic, democracy, demography
derm-	skin	hypodermic, dermatology, epidermis, taxidermy
deus	god	deity, deify
dic(t)	tell, speak	dictum, dictionary, dictation, dictate, dictator, edict, contradict, benediction
dorm-	sleep	dormitory, dormancy, dormant
dox	belief	doxology, paradox, orthodox
duc(t)	lead	seduce, produce, reduce, induce, introduce, conduct
dyna-	power	dynamite, hydrodynamics, dynamic, dynasty
equ-	equal	equitable, equinox, equilibrium, equivalent

Roots

fac-	make, do	manufacture, fact, factory
fer	bear, carry	fertile, ferry, transfer, refer, infer, defer, aquifer
fid	faith, trust	fidelity, confederate, confidence, infidelity, infidel, federal
flu, flux	flowing	influenza, influence, fluid, flush, confluence, fluently, fluctuate
fort-	strong	fortress, fortitude, fort, fortify
fract-	break	refract, infraction, fracture
frater	brother	fraternity, fraternal, fraternize
gen-	race, birth, kind	generate, genetic, eugenics, genesis, genealogy, generation, antigen
geo-	earth	geometry, geography, geocentric, geology, geothermal
greg-	flock, herd	congregation, congregate, gregarious
gress	go	progress, progression, egress
gyn-	woman	gynecology, gynecologist
hetero	different	heterogeneous, heteromorphic, heteronym
homo, homeo	same	homogenize, homogeneous, homonym, homeostasis
homo-	man	homage, Homo sapiens
hydr-	water	hydrate, dehydrate, hydrant, hydraulic, hydrogen, hydrophobia
jac, jec	throw	projectile, projector, eject
lact-	milk	lactose, lactate
junct-	join	juncture, junction, adjunct, conjunction
lat-	side	lateral, equilateral, unilateral
laud	praise	applause, laudable, plausible, applaud
lect-	gather, choose, read	collection, lecture, election, electorate
leg, legis	law	legislate, legal, legislature, legitimize
lith	stone	monolithic, megalith, batholith, Neolithic

Roots

locu, loqu	speak	eloquent, loquacious, colloquial, circumlocution, elocution
log, logy	speech, word, study of	catalogue, dialogue, prologue, psychology, logical, zoology
magn(i)	large, great	magnificent, manufacture, magnate, magnitude, magnum
mal	bad, evil	malnourished, malignant, malicious, malfunction, malcontent,
man, manu	hand	manual, manicure, manacle, maneuver, emancipate, manufacture
meter, metr	measure	meter, barometer, thermometer, symmetry
micro	small	microscope, microwave, micrometer, microbe
mit, miss	send	emit, remit, commit, submit, permit, transmit, mission, permission, missile
mob, mov, mot	move	motor, movie, motivate, emotional, mobile, movie, motivation, emote, immortal
mute	change	mutate, mutation, immutable
nasc, nat	birth, spring forth	nascent, innate, natal, native, renaissance, nativity
nihil, nil	nothing	annihilate
noct-	night	nocturnal
nym	name	antonym, synonym, acronym, pseudonym, homonym, anonymous
oner, onus	burden	onerous, onus
ortho	straight, right, correct	orthopedic, orthodontist, unorthodox, orthodox
pac-	peace	Pacific Ocean, pacify, pacifier, pacifist
path-	feeling, disease	telepathy, sympathy, antipathy, apathy, pathos
pecc-	fault, sin	impeccable, peccadilloes

Roots

ped, pod	foot	pedal, pedestrian, impede, centipede, tripod, podiatry, podium
pel, puls	urge, drive	compel, impel, expel, repel, propel, pulse, impulse, pulsate, compulsory, repulsive
pend, pen	hang	pendulum, pendant, suspend, appendage, pensive, impending
phil-	love	philanthropist, philosophy
phob-	fear	claustrophobia, agoraphobia, homophobia, arachnophobia
phon-	sound	phonograph, telephone, homophone, euphonious, phonetic
photo-	light	photographic, photogenic, photosynthesis
physio-	nature	physiological, physiology
plac	please, appease	placebo, placid, placate, complacent
plen, plete	fill	complete, replenish, plentiful, deplete
pli, plic, plex	fold, bend	complicate, pliable, multiplication
polis	city	metropolis, police, megalopolis, politics, acropolis, Indianapolis
pon, pos	place, put	component, postpone, component, position, deposit, proponent
popul-	people	population, populous, popular
port-	carry	transport, import, export, support, report, portfolio
prec-i	price	precious, depreciate, appreciate
prim-	first, early	primal, primary, primitive, primeval
pseudo-	false	pseudonym, pseudoscience
psych-	mind	psychiatry, psyche, psychology, psychosis
pulmo-	lung	pulmonary
pung-, punct	point	pungent, punctual, puncture
quasi-	like, but not really	quasi-scientific, quasi-official, quasi-war, quasi-corporation

sanct-	holy	sanctuary, sanctimonious, sanction
scien-	know, knowledge	science, conscience, omniscient
scope	sight	microscope, telescope, kaleidoscope, periscope, stethoscope
scrib, script	write	scribe, scribble, inscribe, describe, subscribe, script, manuscript
sequ, secut	follow	consequence, sequence, sequel, consecutive
sol-	alone	solstice, solo, solitary, solitude, solitaire
solv, solut	loosen	solvent, solve, solution, absolve, resolution, resolute, resolve
somn-	sleep	somnambulant, somnolent, somniferous
son-	sound	resonance, resonate, sonic, unison
soph-	wise	sophomore, philosopher, sophisticated
spec(t)	look	spectator, spectacle, aspect, inspect, speculate, respect, prospect, retrospective, expect
spir-	breath, breathe	respirator, aspire, expire, perspire, conspire
string, strict	tighten	stringent, astringent, stricture, strict, restriction, constrict
stru, struct-	build	construct, instruct, destruction, structure
tang, tact, tig	touch	tangible, intangible, tactile, contact, contiguous
tele-	far, far-off	teleport, television, telephone, telegram, telescope, telephoto, telecast, telepathy
tend, tens	hold	contend, pretend, intend, superintendent, tendency, tension
terra-	earth	terrarium, territory, terrain, terrestrial, extraterrestrial, terra firma
theo-	god	theology, atheism, polytheism, monotheism
tom-	cut	anatomy, atom, appendectomy, dichotomy, tonsillectomy, dichotomy
tort-	twist	distortion, torture, retort, distort, contort, torturous
tract-	draw, drag	retractable, attract, tractor, subtract, abstract, extract

Roots

ven(t)	come	ventricle, ventilate, vent, convention, venue, avenue, venture, event, advent, prevent
vert, vers	turn	convertible, controversial, avert, divert, invert, versatile, reversible
vid, vis	see	evidence, providence, video, provide, visual, vista, visit, vision
viv	live	survivor, vivacious, revive, vivid,
voc- (voz, voice)	call, speak, voice	vocabulary, convocation, vocal, vocation, avocation

Latin and Greek Numbers

One	uni	union, unilateral, uniform, university, united
	mono	monotheism, monastic, monotone, monologue
Two	du(o)	duplication, duet, duplex,
	bi	biweekly, bilingual, bicycle, binomial
Three	tri	tricycle, triad, triangle, triceps, trichromatic, triplicate
Four	quad(ri) (ra)	quadruplets, quadruple, quadrangle, quadriceps, quadruped
	tetra	tetragonal, tetrahedron, tetrameter, tetrapod
Five	quin	quintuplet, quintet, quintessence
	pent(a)	pentameter, pentagon, Pentateuch, pentathlon, pentacle, Pentecost
Six	sex	sextant, sexagenarian, sextuplet, sextet
	hex(a)	hexagram, hexadecimal, hexachord, hexagon, hexameter
Seven	sept	septennial, septet, septuagenarian
	hept(a)	heptahedron, heptameter, heptagon
Eight	octo	octagon, octogenarian, octave, octet, octopus
Nine	non	nonagenarian, nonagon
Ten	dec	decagon, decahedron, decade, decalogue, decameter, decimal
One hundred	cent	centipede, centimeter, centennial, century
One thousand	mil-, milli-	milliliter, millimeter, millennium, millipede, milliliter, millisecond

Signal and Transition Words

Description/ List/	Sequence	Comparison/ Contrast	Cause and Effect	Problem/ Solution
for example	first, second, third	however	because	
such as	in the first place	but	since	
to illustrate	first of all	as well as	therefore	
for instance	then	on the other hand	consequently	
in addition	before	while	as a consequence	
and	after	although	in order that	
again	last	different from	so that	
moreover	meanwhile	less than; fewer than	as a result	
also, too	now	also, too	then	
furthermore	finally	like	if...then	
another	for one thing	though	thus	
first of all	next	much as	due to	
second	subsequent (-ly)	yet	accordingly	
additionally	late	similarly	for this reason	
not only...but also		similar to		
		whereas		
		as opposed to		
		still		
		in contrast		

Generic Sentence Starters

Purpose	Sentence Starters
Summarizing	I learned… Today I realized… I still wonder… The most significant thing I learned today was… I would summarize my learning today by saying… My initial thought was_____, and now I am thinking _____ because…
Sharing	I feel… In my opinion… I predict that… I agree/disagree that… My view on the matter is _____ because… My initial reaction is _____ because…
Justifying	I think _____ because… I agree/disagree with _____ because… _____ proves that… Another idea might be _____ because… I was thinking that _____ should be… _____ corroborates the idea that….
Accessing Prior Knowledge	I already know… _____ reminds me of… My experience… I would like to know more about… I would compare _____ to _____ because… Discussing _____ made me consider…
Elaborating	_____ is important because… I chose _____ because… The answer might also be _____ because… I would agree/disagree with _____ because… Another reason could be …. I would add _____ because…

Bibliography

Burke, J. (2002). *Tools for Thought*. Portsmouth, NH: Heinemann.

Dutro, S., & Moran, C. (2003). "Rethinking English Language Instruction: An Architectural Approach." In G. G. García (Ed.), *English Learners: Reaching the Highest Level of English Literacy* (pp.227–258). Newark, DE: International Reading Association.

Echevarria, J., Vogt, M., & Short, D. (2008). *Making Content Comprehensible. The Sheltered Instruction Observation Protocol*. Boston, MA: Pearson.

Eyraud, K., Giles, G., Koenig, S., & Stoller, F. (2000). "The Word Wall Approach: Promoting L2 Vocabulary Learning." *English Teaching Forum*, 38, 2-11.

Head, M. & Readence, J. (1986). *Anticipation Guides: Meaning through Prediction*. In Dishner, E., Bean,T., Readence, J. & Moore, D. (Eds.) (1986). *Reading in the Content-areas*. Dubuque, IA: Kendall/Hunt.

Frayer, D., Frederick, W. C., and Klausmeier, H. J. (1969). *A Schema for Testing the Level of Cognitive Mastery*. Madison, WI: Wisconsin Center for Education Research.

Gibbons, P. (2002). *Scaffolding Language, Scaffolding Learning*. Portsmouth, NH: Heinemann.

Johnson, D. & Johnson, R. (1995). *Creative Controversy: Intellectual Challenge in the Classroom (3rd ed.)*. Edina, MN: Interaction Book Company.

Kagan, S. (1990). *Cooperative Learning for Students Limited in Language Proficiency*. In Brubacher, M., Payne, R. & Rickett, K. (Eds.) (1990). *Perspectives on Small Group Learning*. Ontario, Canada: Oakville.

Kagan, S. (1992). *Cooperative Learning*. San Juan Capistrano, CA: Kagan Cooperative Learning.

Kenfield, K. Unpublished workshop handout.

Krashen, S.D. (2000). *The SSR Handbook: How to Organize and Manage a Sustained Silent Reading Program* (pp. vii-xi). Portsmouth, NH: Heinemann.

Lyman, F.T. (1981). *The Responsive Classroom Discussion: The Inclusion of All Students*. In Anderson, A. (Ed.), *Mainstreaming Digest* (pp.109-113). College Park, MD: University of Maryland Press.

Macon, J., Bewell, D., & Vogt, M. (1991). *Responses to Literature*. Newark, DE: International Reading Association.

Marzano, R. (2004). *Building Academic Background*. Alexandria, VA: MCREL, ASCD.

Marzano, R., Pickering, D. J., & Pollock, J.E. (2001). *Classroom Instruction That Works*. Alexandria, VA: MCREL, ASCD.

Pauk, W. (2005). *How to Study in College (8th Ed.)* Boston, MA: Houghton Mifflin.

Samway, K. (2006). *When English Language Learners Write: Connecting Research to Practice*. Portsmouth, NH: Heinemann.

Seidlitz, J. & Perryman, B., (2008). *Seven Steps to Building an Interactive Classroom: Engaging All Sudents in Academic Conversations*. San Clemente, CA: Canter Press

Seidlitz, J. & Perryman, B., (2011). *Seven Steps to a Language Rich Interactive Classroom: Research-Based Strategies for Engaging All Students*. San Clemente, CA: Canter Press.

Stahl, S.A., & Fairbanks, M.M. (1986). "The Effects of Vocabulary Instruction: A Model-based Meta-analysis." *Review of Educational Research*, 56(1), 72-110.

Taba, H. (1967). *Teachers' Handbook for Elementary Social Studies*. Reading, MA: Addison-Wesley.

Taylor, W. (1953). Cloze Procedure: A New Tool for Measuring Readability. *Journalism Quarterly*. 30, 415-433.

Twain, M. (1986). *The Adventures of Huckleberry Finn: Revised Edition*. New York, NY: Penguin Classics.

Wilhelm, J. (2002). *Action Strategies for Deepening Comprehension*. New York, NY: Scholastic.

Zwiers, J. (2008). *Building Academic Language*. Newark, DE: Jossey-Bass/International Reading Association.

SEIDLITZ PRODUCT ORDER FORM

Three ways to order

- **FAX** completed order form with payment information to **(949) 200-4384**
- **PHONE** order information to **(210) 315-7119**
- **ORDER ONLINE** at **www.seidlitzeducation.com**

Pricing, specifications, and availability subject to change without notice.

PRODUCT	PRICE	QUANTITY	TOTAL
NEW! ELLs in Texas: What Teachers Need to Know 2ND EDITION	$34.95		
NEW! ELLs in Texas: What Administrators Need to Know 2ND EDITION	$29.95		
NEW! Talk Read Talk Write: A Practical Routine for Learning in All Content Areas K-12 2ND EDITION	$32.95		
NEW! Vocabulary Now! 44 Strategies All Teachers Can Use	$29.95		
Diverse Learner Flip Book	$26.95		
ELPS Flip Book	$19.95		
Academic Language Cards and Activity Booklet, ENGLISH	$19.95		
Academic Language Cards, SPANISH	$9.95		
Sheltered Instruction Plus	$19.95		
RTI for ELLs Fold-Out	$16.95		
7 Steps to a Language-Rich Interactive Classroom	$29.95		
7 Pasos para crear un aula interactiva y rica en lenguaje SPANISH	$29.95		
38 Great Academic Language Builders	$24.95		
An Exemplary Disciplinary Alternative Education Program (DAEP) Handbook with CD-ROM	$29.95		
Navigating the ELPS: Using the Standards to Improve Instruction for English Learners	$24.95		
Navigating the ELPS: Math 2ND EDITION	$29.95		
Navigating the ELPS: Science	$29.95		
Navigating the ELPS: Social Studies	$29.95		
Navigating the ELPS: Language Arts and Reading	$34.95		
'Instead Of I Don't Know' Poster, 24" x 36" ENGLISH ☐ Elementary ☐ Secondary	$9.95		
'Instead Of I Don't Know' Poster, 24" x 36" SPANISH (Elementary only)	$9.95		
'Please Speak In Complete Sentences' Poster 24" x 36" ☐ ENGLISH ☐ SPANISH	$9.95		
20 pack 'Instead Of I Don't Know' Posters, 11" x 17" ENGLISH ☐ Elementary ☐ Secondary	$40.00		
20 pack 'Instead Of I Don't Know' Posters, 11" x 17" SPANISH (Elementary only)	$40.00		
20 pack 'Please Speak In Complete Sentences' Posters 11" x 17" ☐ ENGLISH ☐ SPANISH	$40.00		

SHIPPING 9% of order total, minimum $14.95
5-7 business days to ship. If needed sooner please call for rates.
TAX EXEMPT? please fax a copy of your certificate along with order.

DISCOUNT	
SHIPPING	
TAX	
TOTAL	

NAME

SHIPPING ADDRESS   CITY   STATE   ZIP

PHONE NUMBER   EMAIL ADDRESS

TO ORDER BY FAX
to **(949)200-4384**
please complete
credit card info *or*
attach purchase order

☐ Visa ☐ MasterCard ☐ Discover ☐ AMEX

CARD #   EXPIRES
                                   mm/yyyy

SIGNATURE   CVV
                                   3- or 4- digit code

☐ **Purchase Order attached**
please make
P.O. out to
Seidlitz Education

For information about Seidlitz Education products
and professional development, please contact us at

(210) 315-7119 | kathy@johnseidlitz.com
56 Via Regalo, San Clemente, CA 92673
www.seidlitzeducation.com

Giving kids the
gift of **academic
language.**™

REV102116

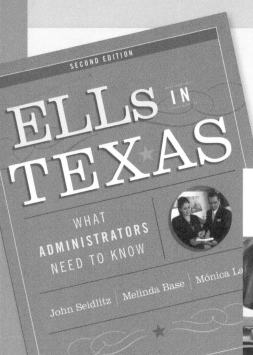

from Seidlitz Education

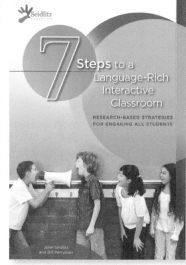

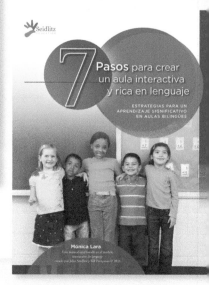

Giving kids
the gift of
academic language.™

Seidlitz
EDUCATION

Information & Ordering
www.seidlitzeducation.com
(210) 315-7119